KOMODO DRAGONS

by Imogen Kingsley

AMICUS | AMICUS INK

Amicus High Interest and Amicus Ink are published by Amicus
P.O. Box 1329, Mankato, MN 56002
www.amicuspublishing.us

Library of Congress Cataloging-in-Publication Data
Title: Komodo dragons / by Imogen Kingsley.
Description: Mankato, Minnesota : Amicus/Amicus Ink, [2019] | Series:
  Lizards in the wild | Audience: K to Grade 3. | Includes index.
Identifiers: LCCN 2018004174 (print) | LCCN 2018006679 (ebook) | ISBN
  9781681515977 (pdf) | ISBN 9781681515595 (library binding) | ISBN
  9781681523972 (paperback)
Subjects: LCSH: Komodo dragon--Juvenile literature.
Classification: LCC QL666.L29 (ebook) | LCC QL666.L29 K57 2019 (print) |
  DDC 597.95/968--dc23
LC record available at https://lccn.loc.gov/2018004174

Photo Credits: iStock/ANDREYGUDKOV, cover, AYImages, 10, tortumasa,
18-19; Shutterstock/Eric Isselee, 2, 22, Victoria Rakhimbaeva, 4-5,
GUDKOV ANDREY, 6, 17, Sergey Uryadnikov, 9, 14-15, kubais, 13, Waddell
Images, 21

Editor: Mary Ellen Klukow
Designer: Peggie Carley
Photo Researcher: Holly Young

Printed in China

HC 10 9 8 7 6 5 4 3 2 1
PB 10 9 8 7 6 5 4 3 2 1

TABLE OF CONTENTS

Not Really a Dragon   4

The Biggest Lizard   7

Where They Live   8

A Meat Eater   11

On the Hunt   12

Deadly Saliva   15

A Fight!   16

On the Lookout   19

Young Dragons   20

A Look at a Komodo Dragon   22

Words to Know   23

Learn More   24

Index   24

NOT REALLY A DRAGON

A Komodo dragon walks
on the beach. He is big.
He has scales. He flicks his
forked tongue. He looks
like a dragon. Is he? No.
He is a lizard.

5

6

THE BIGGEST LIZARD

Wow! He is big! He is the biggest lizard on Earth. A Komodo dragon can grow to be 10 feet (3 m) long. He has a big, flat head. He has a long, strong tail.

WHERE THEY LIVE

Komodo dragons live on a few islands in **Indonesia**. The islands are **remote**. Not many people live there. Parts of the islands are rocky and dry. Parts are grassy.

A MEAT EATER

Most lizards eat both plants and animals. Komodos are carnivores. They only eat meat. They hunt pigs, deer, and **water buffalo**. They also eat dead animals they find.

Check This Out
A Komodo dragon's teeth are hidden behind its gums. They rip flesh.

ON THE HUNT

A female Komodo sees a water buffalo. It is bigger than she is. That is okay. The Komodo dragon is strong. She pounces. She rips with her claws. She bites.

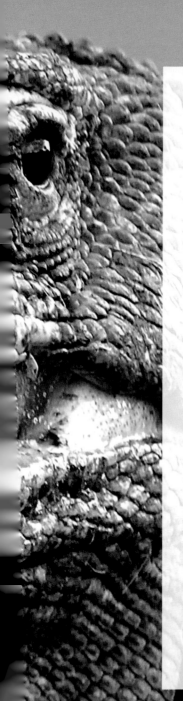

DEADLY SALIVA

The buffalo runs away.
But it will not live. The
Komodo has deadly
saliva. It slowly poisons
its **prey**. The buffalo soon
falls over. The Komodo
dragon eats.

A FIGHT!

Another Komodo wants some food. There is a fight. The Komodos stand on their back legs. Their tails help them balance. They bite. They claw.

Check This Out
Dragons also fight over mates.

ON THE LOOKOUT

After Komodos mate, the female digs a nest. She lays about 25 eggs. She guards her eggs until they hatch.

YOUNG DRAGONS

Young Komodos hatch after nine months. They hunt **rodents** and small lizards. Other animals hunt them. They spend a lot of time in the trees. It is safer there.

A LOOK AT A KOMODO DRAGON

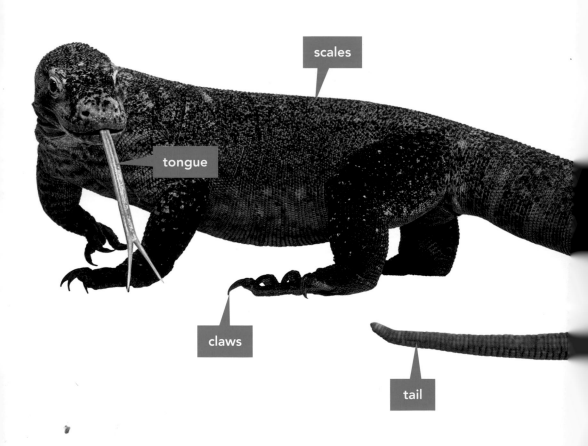

scales

tongue

claws

tail

WORDS TO KNOW

Indonesia A Southeast Asian nation made up of over 18,000 islands.

prey Animals hunted for food by other animals.

remote Far away from people.

rodents Small mammals, like mice.

saliva The liquid in an animal's mouth.

water buffalo A big cow-like animal with horns.

LEARN MORE

Books

Hirsch, Rebecca E. *Komodo Dragons: Deadly Hunting Reptiles*. Minneapolis: Lerner Publishing Group, 2016.

Meister, Cari. *Komodo Dragons*. Minneapolis: Jump!, 2016.

Statts, Leo. *Komodo Dragons*. Minneapolis: Abdo Zoom, 2017.

Websites

DK Find Out!: Lizards
https://www.dkfindout.com/us/animals-and-nature/reptiles/lizards

National Geographic Kids: The Komodo Dragon
https://kids.nationalgeographic.com/animals/komodo-dragon

San Diego Zoo: The Komodo Dragon
http://kids.sandiegozoo.org/animals/komodo-dragon

INDEX

claws, 12, 16

deer, 11

eggs, 19

Indonesia, 8
islands, 8

nest, 19

people, 8, 12
pig, 11

scales, 4

tail, 7, 16
tongue, 4

water buffalo, 11, 12